EDGAR RICE BURROUGHS
Creator of Tarzan

World Writers

EDGAR RICE BURROUGHS
Creator of Tarzan

William J. Boerst

BIO BURR,ed

**MORGAN
REYNOLDS**
Incorporated

Greensboro

EDGAR RICE BURROUGHS: CREATOR OF TARZAN

Copyright © 2000 by William J. Boerst

Photographs Courtesy of EDGAR RICE BURROUGHS, INC.
© 2000 EDGAR RICE BURROUGHS, INC.
Used by Permission.

Library of Congress Cataloging-in-Publication Data

Boerst, William J.
    Edgar Rice Burroughs : Creator of Tarzan / William J. Boerst.--1st ed.
        p. cm. -- (World writers)
    Includes bibliographical references and index.
    ISBN 1-883846-56-0 (lib. bdg.)
        1. Burroughs, Edgar Rice, 1875-1950--Juvenile literature. 2. Novelists, American--20th
century--Biography--Juvenile literature. 3. Adventure stories--Authorship--Juvenile
literature. 4. Tarzan (Fictitious character)--Juvenile literature. [1. Burroughs, Edgar Rice,
1875-1950. 2. Authors, American.] I. Title. II. Series.

PS3503.U687 Z56 2000
813'.52--dc21
[B]
                                                                    00-041847

Printed in the United States of America
First Edition

With love to Robin and Julie.

Contents

Edgar Rice Burroughs

Chapter One

A Rebel Reforms

When Ed Burroughs was sixteen years old, he ran away from the Michigan Military Academy. He found it hard to follow his school's strict rules and had repeatedly been in trouble with authorities. He wrote about this adventure years later:

> I sneaked out of barracks at dusk and walked four and half miles to Pontiac [Michigan]. I crept fearfully through the woods, for all the time I heard the cavalry pursuing me, my budding imagination being strong even then. In Pontiac I hung around the railroad yards waiting for the Chicago train. Every man I saw was a detective searching for me and when the train pulled in and the inspectors passed along with their flares, I knew they were looking for me, but I hid between two freight cars until the train started.

The imaginative Ed arrived home in Chicago on April

15, 1892. He complained to his parents about the "unfair discipline" he received at the academy. The next day a telegram came from Commandant Charles King, which stated: "Your son deserted Thursday. Letter will follow."

In the following letter, King recalled several incidents of Ed's bad behavior. Once, for example, while confined to his quarters, Ed escaped through a window, intent on returning home by rail. That time he had not succeeded. The next time he got away.

Ed's complaints about military school discipline did not earn much sympathy from his father. Major George Tyler Burroughs was a demanding man who ran his household in a military fashion, even requiring meals to be served exactly on the hour. Major Burroughs told Ed that he could decide whether he should return to school. Ed decided to go back and face punishment, which consisted of marching off his misdeeds.

Ed's father had fought in the Civil War as a Union Army major. In February 1863, he married Mary Evaline Zieger in Iowa City, Iowa. After the war, the couple moved to Maine and started a furniture company. This venture lasted until 1868, when the couple, now with two sons, moved to Chicago's West Side and opened a distillery. Before long, there were two more sons. When the distillery burned down, Major Burroughs invested in a battery factory. Then, on September 1, 1875, the fifth son, Edgar Rice Burroughs, was born.

Ed was a bright, alert child. At five years old, he began

Major George Tyler Burroughs ran a strict household.

writing. At age eleven he wrote and illustrated his own poem. He frequently drew cartoons in the margins of textbooks. In 1887, at age twelve, he read *Tales of Ancient Greece*. The mythological stories made a big impression on him.

Ed and his childhood sweetheart, Emma Hulbert, lived on the same street and went to the same public school, Brown School. When he was twelve years old, Ed was removed from Brown School because of a diphtheria scare. His parents had lost two infant sons earlier. They arranged for Ed to attend Mrs. K. S. Cooley's School for Girls, along with a half-dozen other neighborhood boys. His grades there were good. The lowest one was an eighty in composition. In 1888, Ed transferred to Chicago's Harvard School.

Ed's two older brothers, George and Harry, had graduated from engineering school at Yale University in 1889 and gone on to work in their father's battery plant. Then Harry had developed a bad case of tuberculosis, so a job change was called for. The family believed fresh air, sunny weather, and manual labor would help bring Harry's health back. George and Harry purchased Bar Y Ranch in Idaho and moved west.

Between Harvard School's rigid discipline and his father's strict rules, Ed was unhappy. The freedom of rural living and the adventure of being in a new locale lured him west. In the spring of 1891, Ed was given parental permission to go work with his brothers. He later

Ed much preferred life at his brother's ranch over military school.

recalled those days in his *Autobiography*:

> I did chores, grubbed sage brush and drove a team of bronchos to a sultry plow.... Once, after I unhooked them, they ran away and evidently, not being endowed with any too much intelligence, I hung onto the lines after tripping over a sage brush and was dragged around the country three times on my face....

Ed found a black gelding he wanted to tame. Whisky Jack was a wild horse with a bad reputation. He pleaded with the owner until he got permission to try to break him. On the first attempt, the horse jumped twice, then fell on Ed. On the second try, Whisky Jack settled down. After that, he was Ed's horse and only Ed's horse. One of the young rider's jobs was to deliver mail. Through all his experiences around the ranch, Ed became an accomplished horseman.

Idaho offered Ed a taste of adventure. To his dismay, however, Ed's father called him back to Chicago to resume schooling in September. Now the sixteen-year-old was off to Phillips Academy in Andover, Massachusetts.

While at Phillips, Ed worked on the staff of the *Mirror*, his school's literary magazine. He supplied writings and drawings. He was also active in the school's athletic association and became president of his class. Ed was more interested in his social life, however, than in improving his studies. At the end of one term, the principal judged that Ed's academic progress was insufficient. Around the middle of January 1892, he notified the family that Ed would have to withdraw from Phillips.

Mr. Burroughs did not reproach his son but rather welcomed him back home. He had made up his mind that Ed would benefit from even more discipline. He enrolled Ed in the Michigan Military Academy at Orchard Park.

At the Michigan Military Academy the next fall, Ed joined the football team. He enjoyed the sense of belonging and the chance to travel to games at other schools. Eventually, Ed became the team's quarterback, leading them to the title of Champion Prep School Team of the West in June 1895. He was captain two years in a row.

At the end of his first year, after returning from his runaway adventure, Ed was getting more used to military discipline. His schoolwork showed improvement. In December 1892, the superintendent wrote Ed's parents: "Cadet Burroughs has made excellent progress in his studies during the last three months and is satisfactory in discipline. We hope for still better results after Christmas." By this time, Ed had befriended Commandant Charles King.

Ed may have become more disciplined, but he still enjoyed playing pranks. One letter to his parents described how he and two other cadets had short-sheeted another cadet's bed and tied his nightshirt into knots.

Ed became a member of the cavalry troop at the academy and put to use the horsemanship he had learned on the ranch. He wanted to buy his own horse and appealed to his father's sound business instincts by claiming a horse could make them money. Ed's father went along with the idea, and Ed was later riding in competitions. He took second place at the Columbian Saddle Horse Show in April 1893.

A faculty member wrote a letter to Ed's father commending his son's 89.4 percent grade average. But, this did not mean Ed's days as a practical joker were over. He and a classmate, Charles Campbell, were enemies. The two contrived to play a joke based on their well-known rivalry. They staged an argument in front of the other students. Ed slapped Charles's face with his glove. Charles accepted the challenge to a duel with "rifles at fifty paces." The rifles were loaded with blanks, and Ed had hidden a red-ink-soaked handkerchief inside his shirt. Before the event could be carried out, Commandant Charles King heard of it and summoned both boys. When Ed revealed evidence that the entire duel had been a prank, the commandant acted relieved. The other students, however, were angry at being duped and wanted to beat up the two pranksters.

The school's literary magazine, *The Adjutant*, listed Ed as one of the top editors in 1896. The new school newspaper, *The Military Mirror*, may have been his idea; he was listed as one of the editors in its first issue in 1894.

Despite his involvement in extra-curricular activities, Ed still got into trouble. He was accused by the adjutant of neglect of duty and as result was taken down in rank and had privileges curtailed from April 12 through June 10, 1894. Superintendent Rogers wrote Ed's father on April 23 about the specifics of the offense. While he was serving as officer-of-the-day, Ed had supposedly encouraged one cadet to assault another, who had reported the assaulting cadet for breaking a no-smoking rule.

Ed wrote home to present his version of the incident. His friend had been leaning out a window. The student officer on duty assumed the boy was smoking and turned Ed's friend in. The next day, the friend went after the officer to settle the score. Ed negotiated a peace agreement between the two and stopped a fight. Ed turned in his friend for throwing a punch, but he also defended the friend and told the officer that he would have to answer to Ed. Unfortunately, the officer was a pet of school administrators. The other cadets supported Ed and his friend. Still, Ed came dangerously close to being expelled, but because of the younger teachers' support of him, the administrators made his punishment less severe.

Ed was able to redeem himself. By his senior year he had been promoted to captain. When he recalled his Michigan Military Academy undergraduate experiences years later, he was not bitter about his treatment there, and in fact even wondered why he had been as successful as he was, given his difficult behavior.

As Ed approached graduation in 1895, he considered career plans. He wanted to enter military service as an officer, but to do that meant attending West Point Military Academy. Cadets had to be appointed to the academy, and only one appointment per state was allowed a year. His chances to be the Michigan appointee were not good. He asked his brother George to help. George, who was by now a well-known Idaho rancher, sought the cooperation of a member of the U. S. House of Representatives from that state. Ed received an appointment to the academy on one condition: He had to pass an entrance exam.

One hundred eighteen applicants took the test; only fourteen passed. Ed was not among the successful ones. He decided that he would return to Michigan Military Academy as assistant commandant. His duties included acting as a tactical officer, instructing in cavalry and riflery, and teaching geology.

The position did not start until the fall. After working as an ice deliverer for the summer, Ed returned to Michigan Military Academy and his new duties. He had no background for teaching geology, so he studied along with his students. As assistant commandant, he had to enforce discipline, a job he felt well qualified for because as a cadet he had been involved in breaking so many rules.

At one point Ed went too far with his strict discipline. When he was walking through the barracks, some cadets threw something at him. He warned two cadets he found in the hall, but later the same thing happened again. Ed informed the unit that they had to produce the guilty party in twenty-four hours, with no more repeated incidents, or they would all be penalized.

The next night the cadets threw more objects at him. True to his word, Ed made the group go on a two-hour night march. The next day, when the tired students performed poorly in class, faculty members complained about Ed's harsh discipline. Not too long after the faculty complaint, Ed punished the same cadets again for another infringement, this time at midnight. The school administration forbade any further night marches.

Ed felt caught in the middle. He was no longer part of the student body; at the same time, he did not belong with the faculty either. What had seemed like a choice position was turning unpleasant. Despite his difficulties, Ed was able to manage the football and baseball teams, and he advised the school magazine as well. By spring 1896, though, twenty-year-old Ed was tired of school routine and ready for a change.

Chapter Two

A Taste of Army Life

Ed hit on a way out of his situation. He resigned his post at the Michigan Military Academy and attempted to enlist in the army in Detroit. The recruiting officers did not believe that he was twenty-one years old (he was a few months short), so he had to obtain written permission from his father and await clearance to be assigned in an area outside Detroit's jurisdiction.

Ed finally obtained clearance to work with the Seventh Cavalry at Fort Grant, Arizona Territory. Fort Grant was considered "the worst assignment in the United States Army." After a long and difficult train and stagecoach ride, he arrived at the fort on May 23, 1896.

His superiors soon discovered that Ed was an expert rider. This was an asset for a unit designed to protect white settlers from Indian raids. Most enlisted men at Fort Grant, however, spent their time doing hard labor—clearing rocks for road building—not riding out after Apache raiders.

Ed came down with dysentery from contaminated

drinking water and had to spend time in the troop hospital. The treatment prescribed by the army doctors was starvation and big doses of castor oil.

The two doctors on Ed's ward were always drunk, he remembered. "When they made the rounds of the hospital they referred to us as 'this' and 'it.' To them we were less than human beings and if they decided that one of us was dead, we were dead."

These two doctors diagnosed that Ed had a problem with his heart and should be discharged from the army. Eventually, Ed was able to lie his way out of the hospital without the heart diagnosis being filed. Ed had heard that at last the troop would be going out on an assignment. Two settlers had been murdered, supposedly in an Apache raid. Ed's troop was to locate and arrest the offenders.

Ed traveled through the desert still suffering from dysentery. The troop went to the location of the crime over treacherous mountains. At one point, their supply wagon tumbled over the trail's edge and was lost far below. When they arrived at the town, residents locked up their wells and left their dogs loose to attack the men.

Because their supply wagon was gone, the men bought local potatoes and shot jackrabbits. Ed described the meat: "The muscles of those we killed were filled with large white grubworms as big as one's thumb."

The troop never did find the offending Indians and returned to the post empty-handed. Ed was still weak from his bout with dysentery, so his commanding officer took pity and gave him a less demanding duty—stable boy for fourteen horses. One of his jobs was to haul and distribute hay. To give himself a break, Ed would often pile as much hay as possible into the horsecart, then climb into the pile for the ride back to the stables. Sometimes he fell off the load, taking half of it with him.

Ed had always been attracted to drawing and painting. Now with time on his hands, he delighted in sketching his horses. He also drew political cartoons and pictures of everyday life in the army.

When he enlisted, Ed had envisioned a period of adventure followed by commission as an officer, but two months of hard labor, dysentery, and one futile search for an Indian attacker left him disillusioned. At the end of summer 1896, he wrote to his father for help in finding a way out of the army. Ed knew a soldier could buy his way out from his superiors, or request a transfer to a different cavalry unit. These methods did not always work. He wrote his father: "If you think best I will make no attempt to transfer. I made my bed and I will lie in it." During the Christmas season of 1896, he was still in the Arizona Territory.

Ed's father was doing what he could to get his son out of the cavalry. He had two friends write Secretary of War R. A. Alger and plead Ed's case. They argued that his heart condition indicated by the military doctors would prevent him from securing a commission. One friend also referred to Ed's mother's unsubstantiated poor health.

On March 19, 1897, Ed got word from his father that he had been granted a discharge. Once he was out of the service, he looked back carefully at his military record and created this list:

My Wonderful Military Career
1. Right Guard Brown School Cadets
2. High Private Harvard School Cadet
3. Plebe—Orchard Lake
4. Corporal—Orchard Lake
5. Sergeant Major—Orchard Lake
6. 2nd Lieutenant—Orchard Lake
7. Private—Orchard Lake
8. 1st Sergeant—Orchard Lake
9. Captain—Orchard Lake
10. 2nd. Lieutenant Michigan Military Academy
    Tactical Officer, Commandant
11. Private—7th U.S. Cavalry

After leaving the army, Ed accepted a call from his brothers in Idaho to help load cattle in Nogales, Arizona, and transport them by rail to Kansas City. Transporting was difficult work. Ed and one helper supervised seven of their own railroad cars plus others added on during the journey. Because the cattle were malnourished and thirsty, the two cattle herders would have to drag seven or eight dead animals out of each car at stops along the way. Some cattle fell down and had to be "tailed up":

After I had got past their horns and down between them it was not so bad for about the worst they could do was step on me. The old fellow helped me at first, but finally he got kicked so badly that I had to do it alone and with the animals swaying and crowding it was a strenuous job to get an animal back on its feet after it had fallen down. Of course it is physically impossible for a man to lift a steer, but if you get hold of the tail and heave up the natural inclination of the beast is to help itself and about all you do is to balance it while it gets its feet under itself, though at that there is considerable heavy lifting.

By the summer 1897, Ed was back home in Chicago. He had missed his childhood sweetheart, Emma, and decided to renew their courtship. He went to work at his father's business, the American Battery Company, and took classes at the Art Institute of Chicago.

Ed had sworn that once he got home, he would never leave. But, he could not endure a life at the battery company under the persistent eye of his father. He decided to move back to Idaho and work with his brothers on the ranch. But, once out in Idaho, he discovered that the ranch was not doing well. The cattle business had proven to be unsuccessful. The boys were broke.

On February 15, 1898, the U.S.S. *Maine* exploded in Havana Harbor off Cuba. On April 19, Congress declared war on Spain. Suddenly, President McKinley needed 125,000 military troops for combat. Theodore Roosevelt began to organize the Rough Riders. Ed wrote Roosevelt, hoping to be selected. Roosevelt's response was not encouraging: "I wish I could take you in, but I am afraid that the chances of our being over-enlisted forbid my bringing a man from such a distance."

In June 1898, Harry backed Ed in his purchase of a stationery store in Pocatello, Idaho. The store also had a newsstand, a cigar counter, and photo supplies. In addition to his store duties, Ed managed a newspaper route, which he sometimes handled himself.

The business did not succeed. Ed lacked enough capital to build the business over an extended period. Ed's habit of beginning a project with enthusiasm and then losing interest may have been a factor, too. At year's end, the former owner bought the store back. Later, Ed remarked, "God never intended me for a retail merchant!"

The question for Ed was simple: what precisely did God intend him to do? During his stationery-store days, he did some writing. Two of his poems appeared in the local newspaper. One, a satire about African-American servitude, foreshadowed one of his later themes: how civilization destroys both humans and nature.

Once Ed left the stationery store, he helped his brothers herd cattle. Most of all he enjoyed working with horses. He believed that the American practice of breaking horses removed their spirit, whereas the European practice of training horses kept it intact. As a rule, Ed found that cattle herders tortured horses instead of treating them kindly.

When spring roundup was over, there was no more work at the ranch, so Ed tried to secure a commission in a volunteer army, but the plan to organize the volunteer army was soon abandoned. He had no choice but to return to his father's battery company in Chicago. There he started at the bottom and began to work his way up.

Ed had never given up on having a future with Emma Hulbert. He first proposed to her at age fourteen. He pursued her for the next ten years. Emma's parents were not fond of Ed. They saw his fickle past as a sign of future instability. Finally her parents gave in, and the couple wed in Chicago on January 31, 1900. A few days later, Emma's father passed away at age seventy-one.

Ed tried to support the two of them on his twenty-dollar-a-week salary, but it was difficult. He disliked working under his father's supervision, and was especially envious that his brothers were living the free life in Idaho while he was stuck in the plant.

Since Ed's brothers had made little money in their cattle venture, they decided to launch a new career. They had observed gold miners along the Snake River. The two brothers, and their friend Lewis Sweetser, were all engineering graduates from the Sheffield Scientific School of Yale University. They saw the panning methods as slow and laborious. They wondered why miners couldn't use suction to dredge the river bottom. In 1897, they built

Ed married his childhood sweetheart, Emma Hulbert, on January 31, 1900.

their first dredging machine and formed a mining company. For the workers, they built a two-story houseboat that contained eighteen rooms, including a thirty-by-fifteen-foot living room. The boat could house all the workers and their families.

The dredge vacuumed up soil and gravel from the river bottom and deposited it on burlap-covered tables. Gold would catch in the burlap while the rest of the mixture sieved through. The company hired a crew of four and then built a separate houseboat for themselves.

Meanwhile, back in Chicago, Ed was experimenting with writing and art during his spare time. For his niece Evelyn, he wrote booklets of verses illustrated with cartoons. Along with the verses were recipes and instructions for making finger-puppet plays.

Finally, in 1903, Ed got what he had been waiting for—an invitation to become part of his brothers' Idaho dredging operation. He and Emma paid for the trip through loans from his brother Coleman. The two packed up everything they owned and shipped it west. On the journey, by train and stagecoach, Ed was impressed with what he saw:

> Stanley Basin is in the heart of the Sawtooth Mountains, the most beautiful spot in the United States. There granite peaks rise far above the timber line and the summits of the higher mountains are covered with perpetual snow, while nestled

in the valleys is a series of beautiful lakes and numerous mountain streams.

Their first home in the Stanley Basin was a tent. Later they built a cabin on shore. After little luck in Stanley Basin, the company established itself in two other locations—Stanley Creek in Idaho's Sawtooth Mountains and Snake River in Oregon. Ed and Emma went to work with Harry in Oregon after Ed and George had begun to quarrel over who was doing more work.

On the way to Parma, Idaho, near the Oregon dredging location, Ed tried to increase their savings of forty dollars by gambling. Instead of winning, he lost it all. Harry had to send him enough money to reach Parma.

Ed began to draw again at Parma. He also wrote his first fiction piece, "Mindoka, 937th Earl of One Mile Series M. An Historical Fairy Tale." He wrote the eighty-two page satirical tale on company letterhead, the back of the American Genealogical Society of Chicago, and even some old phone bills.

Ed was elected trustee of Parma. He won by one vote—49 to 48. His vote-getting method was very straightforward. He stopped people and asked them to vote for him so that he would not end up with zero votes in his favor. Apparently, a lot of people wanted to help save him from that embarrassment. Before Ed could carry out the tasks of his newly won office, the dredging business went bankrupt. Creditors' notes came due without any way of paying them.

Harry knew a friend in Salt Lake City, Utah, who worked for the Oregon Short Line Railroad Company. The friend offered Ed a job as railroad policeman and even sent train tickets for him and Emma, who had no money of their own. In April 1904, they left Parma for Salt Lake City. His official outfit consisted of "a blue uniform with gleaming brass buttons and . . . a club." His main job was to keep indigents out of the yards and railroad cars.

Ed's meager salary forced the couple to live frugally. Ed volunteered to help by doing the laundry:

> I took all of our soiled clothes and put them in the bathtub, turned the water on them and let them soak over night. I did not know until next morning that I should have separated the white clothes from the colored ones and thereafter it would have made no difference since they were all colored.

In addition to laundering, Ed put new soles on his shoes and made his own beer.

Chapter Three

Finding a Career

Ed and Emma wearied of trying to live on a railroad policeman's salary. After five months, Ed resigned his job. To pay their way back to Chicago, they sold all their household possessions. The sale was successful and they rode back home first class.

In Chicago, Ed obtained work as a timekeeper on a construction site. The building was many stories high. Ed worked on the steel girders in the open air, an unfortunate location because he was afraid of heights. He did not last long at that job. During the next weeks, he had several short term positions. He was a door-to-door salesman, and he peddled electric light bulbs and candy to businesses.

In the paper, he noticed an ad for "expert accountant." He didn't know what an accountant did, but he applied anyway and got the job. The employer soon made Ed his office manager, a position Ed kept for two years.

Ed had never really given up the dreams of having a military commission or of being a cavalry instructor. In March 1906, he sent out several letters inquiring about such opportunities. One inquiry went to his old commandant and mentor at Michigan Military Academy, Charles King. To Ed, King symbolized the best a person could be. Ed admired his "forthrightness, attitude of simple humility, and emphasis upon principle and justice."

At a suggestion from another former Michigan Military Academy commandant, Fred Smith, Ed wrote the Chinese Imperial Reform Association in Chicago and the Imperial Chinese Delegation in Washington asking for a position in the Chinese Army. Both organizations replied that they were not looking for military men.

In 1907, Sears, Roebuck and Company placed Ed in its correspondence department. He soon became the manager of its stenographic department. He oversaw 150 stenographers and typists in one large room. It was good that Ed had found steady employment. Emma was pregnant with their first child.

Emma gave birth to their daughter, Joan, in January 1908. But, in August, just as they had settled into a routine, Ed quit Sears, Roebuck to form his own business. He left the company with an excellent work record and an invitation to return in the future.

Ed formed a partnership with a man named Dentzer. They called themselves advertising contractors. They trained potential salespeople through correspondence courses to sell aluminum pots and pans. The idea was that, once trained, the salespeople would sell the pots and pans for "Burroughs & Dentzer, Advertising Contractors" and then send them the proceeds. In reality, most trainees quit when it came to the actual selling, often neglecting to send in either their earnings or the remaining pots and pans. The business soon folded.

Emma gave birth to a son, Hulbert, in August 1909. Ed had secured a position as office manager for the Physicians Co-operative Association. The proprietor, Dr. Stace, had invented what he claimed was a cure for alcoholism. Ed wrote a series of booklets instructing on how to sell Dr. Stace's medicine door to door. About this time, his former boss at Sears, Roebuck offered Ed his old job back, but Ed decided against it. Of that decision, he recalled: "I would probably have been fixed for life with a good living salary, yet if I had, the chances are that I should never have written a story, which proves that occasionally it is better to do the wrong thing than the right thing."

Soon, the Stace-Burroughs partnership dissolved and times became hard indeed. His lunches consisted of a few ginger snaps. The couple pawned their jewelry. At Christmastime, to cut expenses, Ed drew their own cards and wrote humorous verses inside each one.

Ed's next job was as an agent supervising the sale of lead pencil sharpeners. This business did not prove successful either, but it was a turning point in Ed's career nevertheless. During his time on the job, Ed had long periods of free time that he filled by reading pulp magazines. "Pulps" were low-budget magazines printed on cheap, rough paper. "There were several all-fiction publications among them—some that I had never seen before," he explained. "I remember thinking that if other people got money for writing such stuff I might, too, for I was sure I could write stories just as rotten as theirs." In July 1911, he began writing his second story. But, this time he had a definite market in mind.

Once the lead pencil business folded, Ed went to work for his brother Coleman, who now owned a stationery company. He continued to write on the job, however, and sent the first half of "A Princess of Mars" to *Argosy Magazine* in August 1911. The story tells of a soldier who wakes up from a trance and finds himself in the middle of the Martian civilization Ed called Barsoom.

Ed knew nothing about how the publishing business worked. As he put it, "I had never met an editor, or an author or a publisher. I had no idea how to submit a story or what to expect in payment. Had I known anything about it at all I would not have thought of submitting half a novel." To his amazement, *Argosy* accepted "A Princess of Mars." Even more shocking was the fact they offered to pay $400. Now convinced that he should write for a living, Ed started a second story. He also became a manager of *System*, a business magazine.

Thomas Newell Metcalf was the editor of *Argosy*'s

sister magazine, *All-Story*. He asked Ed to write a novel set in medieval times. If it was acceptable, Metcalf agreed to run it as a serial. Three weeks later Ed had completed a book-length manuscript he called "The Outlaw of Torn," but Metcalf rejected it. Ed sent a revision back to Metcalf, who rejected that also.

Despite this discouraging setback, Ed continued to write fiction. In a letter to Metcalf in March 1912, Ed described a new story he was working on:

> The story I am on now is of the scion of a noble English house—of the present time—who was born in tropical Africa where his parents died when he was about a year old. The infant was found and adopted by a huge she-ape, and was brought up among a band of fierce anthropoids.
>
> The mental development of this ape-man in spite of every handicap, of how he learned to read English without knowledge of the spoken language, of the way in which his inherent reasoning faculties lifted him high above his savage jungle friends and enemies, of his meeting with a white girl, how he came at last to civilization and to his own, makes most fascinating writing and I think will prove interesting reading, as I seem especially adapted to the building of the "damphool" species of narrative.

Metcalf was interested in this new idea and Ed began the manuscript in December 1911. He finished it in May 1912 and mailed it in June. In return, Metcalf mailed Ed a check for $700 and wasted little time running the story. He liked it so much that he changed his editorial policy. Instead of running it serially over several months, the entire October 1912 issue of *All-Story* was devoted to "Tarzan of the Apes."

Ed had used the pen name "Normal Bean" with his first two published stories. He wanted the name to suggest the writer had an everyday, average mind. The editors mistook the word "Normal" for a misspelling and printed "Norman" instead. It killed the joke so Ed began publishing under his full name, Edgar Rice Burroughs.

The Tarzan story was a success. Ed was now receiving attention from critics, who were curious about what other fiction had influenced Ed's ideas. One suggestion was the adventure stories of Sir Arthur Conan Doyle, the creator of Sherlock Holmes. Another suggested influence was H.G. Wells, who had published eleven science fiction and fantasy novels by the time "A Princess of Mars" appeared. Ed also greatly admired the adventure writer Jack London.

Ed first claimed that the idea for "Tarzan of the Apes" began with the Roman legend of Romulus and Remus, the two founders of Rome who were said to have been raised by a wolf. Another obvious influence was Rudyard Kipling's *The Jungle Book*, which Ed had read as a young

All-Story published Ed's first Tarzan story in 1912.

man. But, Ed's best explanation for the how he arrived at the idea behind the Tarzan character and story was his own imagination: "I find I can write better about places I've never seen than those I have seen."

"Tarzan of the Apes" was filled with many classical themes. It featured conflict between heredity and environment, a lone man pitted against nature, and the search for individual freedom. It added a new twist to the ongoing debate over the destructive qualities of civilization versus the simple virtues of nature and its creatures.

The story received some criticism. One problem was the occasional errors, such as Sabor the tiger. Many readers, unlike Ed, were aware that tigers are not native to Africa, and they pointed this out in letters to *All-Story*. Later, in the book version, Ed corrected his error by changing Sabor to a lioness.

As he had done with "A Princess of Mars," in "Tarzan of the Apes" Ed used an indeterminate ending to leave open the possibility of writing a sequel. Metcalf received many letters from readers hungry for more Tarzan adventures. He asked Ed if he would write one. Remembering his failure with "The Outlaw of Torn," Ed hesitated. He had another project to complete, a sequel to "A Princess of Mars" he called "The Gods of Mars." He mailed it to Metcalf in October 1912. He also inquired at the A. C. McClurg publishing company about making "Tarzan of the Apes" into a book. As an enticement, he mentioned supportive letters sent to *All-Story* about his Tarzan tale.

McClurg rejected politely. When he submitted to another publishing house, Bobs-Merrill, he offered to send copies of some fan letters. Bobs-Merrill rejected the proposal, too, and two other companies arrived at similar conclusions.

Chapter Four

From Pulps to Books

Editor Metcalf suggested an idea for Ed's sequel to "Tarzan of the Apes." Why not transplant Tarzan to some center of civilization, like New York City, and have him react to the ways of the civilized world? Ed latched on to this suggestion and had Tarzan visit Paris. When he sent Metcalf his outline for the sequel, his editor had only two suggestions. One was to figure a way around his all-too-frequent shipwreck device. The other was to change the geographical emphasis from Paris back to the African jungle. Ed agreed to carry out both suggestions.

Metcalf found another problem when he received the completed story, called "The Ape Man." He felt it needed more balance and rejected it.

Ed responded to Metcalf's criticism: "Sorry you don't like the Ape-Man. I put a lot of work on it. You approved of the plans, and I did not deviate from them except in such minor details as seemed necessary."

Metcalf held his ground and rejected "The Ape Man."

Ed then sent it to Street and Smith's *New Story Magazine*, which promptly paid him $1000 and changed the title to "The Return of Tarzan."

In February 1913, the Burroughses' third child, John, was born. That same month, Ed's father passed away. Although Ed had fond memories of his father, he also felt relieved to be free from his scrutiny. He had always felt that he did not quite measure up to his father's expectations. Fortunately for Ed, his father had seen him succeed as a writer before his death. In future diary entries, he would write "Father's birthday today" or "My father was born in Warren, Massachusetts 107 years ago today."

After hearing that "The Ape Man" would be published in *New Story*, Metcalf was upset. He wrote Ed that he was surprised that he had not made the revisions and resubmitted it to *All-Story*. Metcalf said that "somehow your course of action doesn't strike me as having been friendly."

Ed was puzzled by the editor's displeasure, but responded politely by pointing out that "The Ape Man" had been submitted to *All-Story* first because of his loyalty to Metcalf as a friend.

Ed was determined to have more than one market for his stories. He sent a new story called "The Inner World" to the upscale slick, *American Magazine*, whose editor had requested to see some of Ed's writings. It was no surprise when the editor wrote that he could not use the piece. It was simply too wild for the conservative readers of *American Magazine*. Compared to the pulps, "slicks" were printed on expensive slick paper and catered to more intellectual and literary readers.

Metcalf and Ed resolved their differences when the editor proposed a plan. Metcalf would receive first refusal on any of Ed's stories, and he could request a reasonable amount of revision. Ed produced a counter proposal demanding five cents a word and limiting him to one revision per story. Metcalf countered again with two cents a word, and Ed agreed.

At Metcalf's suggestion, Ed detailed the Barsoomian geography left sketchy in "A Princess of Mars." He supplied the editor with a map and a glossary of Martian terms to be run in a single issue of the magazine. Critics noted that Barsoomian mythology paralleled that of Egyptian mythology. His goddess Issus sounds similar to the Egyptian goddess Isis. His Lost Sea of Korus echoes the son of Isis, named Horus.

A new moneymaking possibility arose when Munsey magazines, the umbrella company that owned *Argosy* and *All-Story*, arranged for the serialization of "Tarzan of the Apes" in the *New York Evening World*. After this success, the *New York Evening World* agreed to pay Ed $300 for syndication rights to "The Ape Man." He also arranged a syndication agreement with *Cleveland Press* and was assured that he would have future agreements with the *New York Evening World* for other pieces.

In March 1913, Ed sent a story called "The Cave Girl" to Metcalf. He made sure he gave over first serial rights

Ed had not considered a writing career until his late thirties.

only. That way he was in a position to pursue syndication rights on his own. He arranged with an agent to handle most of his syndication rights.

Ed had sold four of five completed stories. He decided that because magazine serialization of his stories was progressing at a regular pace, the next step was to find book publishers. He contacted publishers Reilly and Britton about "Tarzan of the Apes," but they declined. Next, he went to Rand McNally of Chicago. They talked with him but, in the end, also rejected the manuscript.

Critics complained about Ed's use of unbelievable incidents to propel his story line. But, the pulp-fiction market demanded rapid writing and quick resolutions. For the sake of time, Ed had faith that his audience was willing to suspend disbelief. He was learning the tricks necessary to keep people reading. His fans were thrilled by the tremendous breadth of Ed's imagination. He had a talent for creating unusual characters and locations. He created red, green, black, white, and yellow Martians. He described caves that ran through the ice near Mars's North Pole to a green valley. Among unusual animals, he created a bull-sized hornet called the "sith," and the "apt," a hairy, white monster with four legs and two hands.

A. R. Sessions, editor of *New Story*, wanted to see some of Ed's material. Ed was still sitting on "The Outlaw of Torn," and sent it to him. Sessions came back with a low offer. He and Ed continued to dicker until they finally reached an agreement: $500 for "Outlaw," but if readers liked it, Ed would get another two cents per word.

Ed carried his business knowledge over to the writing field. He knew he was in demand, so he made careful decisions. He tried setting his own prices for stories. Although he was a careful businessman, Ed was still impulsive. Once he had tasted success, he purchased an automobile. Then he decided to relocate to California. He rationalized the move to his editors by saying that the Chicago winters were too harsh for his children.

The cross-country trip, with three small children between the ages of six months and five years old, was long and hard. Roads in 1913 were inadequately paved or not paved at all. There were few gas stations and no fast-food restaurants.

Ed continued to write. He had sent Metcalf a realistic story called "The Mucker." It came back with a rejection and the comment: "I might say that I don't think the story balances." "The Mucker" dealt with a now favorite theme of Ed's: how a flawed character improves once he has encountered such reforming influences as country living and romantic love. Ed reused another idea: lost heritage. In this case, the protagonists were descendants of an ancient Japanese dynasty. The story was also rejected at *New Story*. Ed decided to revise it. He shortened the story and tightened its progression before submitting it again to *All-Story*.

Meanwhile, he kept on with other projects. *All-Story* was preparing to increase publishing frequency from a monthly to a weekly. Its editor offered to accept "...all manner of stuff, novels 30,000 to 40,000 words long, serials, and short stories." Once "The Mucker " had been revised, Metcalf purchased it for $1,450, the largest amount for a Burroughs story yet.

In January 1914, Ed began to write his third Tarzan story. When he was finished, he sent it off, not to just one publisher, but to two. Ed had learned a lesson: he could usually get more money if he played editors off one another. He submitted to both *All-Story* and *New Story*, which prompted a series of telegrams in a battle over the manuscript. Eventually, it sold for $2,000, $550 more than the he received for "The Mucker."

It was unusual for an author to pit one editor against another. Even more unusual was that when Sessions lost his copy of the manuscript, Ed asked Metcalf to mail his copy to the competitor, which Metcalf did. Ed's training in shrewd business deals was paying off in his new career as a pulp writer.

Chapter Five

Wanderlust

Ed and Metcalf had a misunderstanding over serial rights. Metcalf thought that he had paid for all serial rights for "The Beasts of Tarzan." Meanwhile, Metcalf moved to *Argosy,* and Robert H. Davis came to the newly formed *All-Story-Cavalier* weekly magazine.

In his dealings with both Metcalf and Davis, Ed was determined to release only first serial rights. At one point, he even threatened to stop writing until he got his way. Davis wrote to Ed that the company was officially giving him back all except first serial rights.

The editor at the *New York Evening World,* Albert Payson Terhune, negotiated with Ed for newspaper rights to a story called "The Eternal Lover." Ed asked one cent a word. Terhune complained that it would be three times what they had paid for "The Return of Tarzan" and ten times what they had paid for "Tarzan of the Apes." Ed countered that his stories were worth more now than they had been earlier. The two compromised on $200.

Financially, Ed was doing quite well by the summer

of 1913. He had made $4,600 in story sales. He had earned an additional $6000 in commissions through syndications. In all, he had $10,600 to his credit, a fair amount in the early 1900s. As the family prepared for a return trip to Chicago, he purchased a new car.

As his first stint in California ended, Ed penned two very different stories. "The Girl from Farris's" was a realistic novel dealing with corruption in large cities. "The Lad and the Lion" was another Tarzan adventure.

At last, book publication of "Tarzan of the Apes" seemed imminent. A. C. McClurg and Company, which had rejected "Tarzan of the Apes" earlier, asked to see the manuscript again. As negotiations moved ahead, Ed turned everything over to agent William Chapman. With heightening tension in Europe at the approach of World War I, Ed's dream of becoming a war correspondent was revived. He realized, however, after applying for a position as a correspondent with Terhune that the idea had been a hasty one. He was a married man with a family. He withdrew his application. In May 1914, a final agreement was reached with McClurg about the book version of "Tarzan of the Apes."

Ed and Emma now had three children: Six-year-old Joan, five-year-old Hulbert, and one-year-old John, now called Jack. Ed was developing a writing routine around his home duties. He was an active parent. It was not unusual for him to be typing away while one or more of his children crawled around his legs or sat nearby. A typical day at home involved the kids playing and laughing with the family's Airedale terrier, Tarzan. Although Ed lacked musical talent, he enjoyed listening to marches and hymns. Emma had once trained to become a singer, so she encouraged the children to sing and play the piano.

Ed was usually at his desk by seven or seven-thirty in the morning. He would work until noon, have lunch, and then work an hour or two more. He followed this routine five or six days a week. Occasionally, he worked evenings, particularly if he happened to be revising. Ed only did deep revision on a yarn if an editor requested it; otherwise, he worked on a final copy, reflecting on each sentence before writing it. He was not one to wait for inspiration to strike. Instead, he simply sat and wrote what came. His typing method was hunt-and-peck. Daily output averaged about ten to twelve double-spaced pages.

Ed frequently had nightmares. When these occurred, he moaned or cried aloud. Emma soothed him back to sleep. Another recurring nighttime problem was neuritis in his left shoulder. Some nights he would pace the floor in pain. For years, he suffered with this ailment.

Ed loved automobiles and motoring excursions. He enjoyed tennis, golf, and baseball, and of course, horseback riding. As for mixing socially at parties, he had little time for that. He was neither a conversationalist nor a good listener. His son Hulbert always maintained that the root of his apparent boredom at large social events was actually shyness.

In April 1914, Ed began writing "Thuvia, Maid of Mars." Robert Davis at *All-Story-Cavalier* wanted to confer with Ed about his work. The one-day meeting was scheduled in New York City. Davis knew how to get along with Ed better than Metcalf had. The two editors were different types. Metcalf had his roots in the eastern Ivy League establishment. Like Ed, Davis came from the Midwest, and they both shared a dry sense of humor. At the same time, he was a no-nonsense editor who would not tolerate carelessness.

Davis suggested that Ed slow his writing pace to avoid mistakes and to keep from exhausting himself. But, because payment was based on word count, Ed naturally kept his attention on writing longer stories. Excessive requests for revisions cost him money. On the other hand, his revised stories were usually longer than the originals, which ended up costing his publishers more money.

During the nine months following the Burroughses' return to Chicago from California, Ed completed five stories. In one, he introduced the idea of an automatic pilot. He also invented the "obstruction evader," a device that used diffuse radioactive rays to detect barriers much like the yet-to-be-invented radar. His Phantom Bowmen of Lothar were created from the Lotharians' mental concentration. On a planet with scarce water and food resources, the people of Lothar also maintained their bodies through auto-suggested dietary procedures.

In "Barney Custer of Beatrice," Ed's sequel to "The

From left to right, Hulbert, Emma, John and Joan Burroughs.

Mad King," he inserted coincidences to make the story work, such as overheard conversations, a bullet from a firing squad only creasing the hero's skull, and look-alike characters. But, Ed also used some new ideas. One was the creation of an Earth-type airplane that used parachutes.

In 1914, Ed wrote 400,000 words, or eight stories. "The Lad and the Lion" was the shortest one at 40,000 words. "Pellucidar," a story set in the Earth's core, was the longest at 60,000 words. Others that year included "The Beasts of Tarzan," "The Girl from Farris's," "Thuvia, Maid of Mars," "The Cave Man," "Sweetheart Primeval," and "Barney Custer of Beatrice."

Ed was becoming interested in the silent motion picture industry. In January, he signed an agreement with William Selig from the Chicago-based motion-picture company Polyscopes for "The Lad and the Lion" and another story he was still working on called "Ben, King of Beasts." Ed would receive $800 from the two movies. The movie version of "The Lad and the Lion" came out in May 1917. It did not faithfully follow the book in every respect, but it did preserve the main parts.

By the summer of 1916, Ed was exhausted from his heavy writing schedule. He was also bothered by the worsening neuritis in his left shoulder. He prescribed himself an unusual remedy: An auto tour to Maine. He ordered supplies from Sears, Roebuck for the trip: "folding beds and camp chairs, kerosene oil-gas stove, 50 yards of canvas," and four pieces of mosquito netting. He planned to drive through Coldwater, Michigan, where Emma's family had a vacation retreat; Orchard Lake, where Michigan Military Academy was located; Portland, Maine; and Warren, Massachusetts, Ed's father's birthplace. From Bangor, Maine, the group would head south to Portland, into New Hampshire, then on to New York City and Washington before heading back to the Midwest. The entire family embarked on the journey— Ed, Emma, and their three children. Their maid and chauffeur accompanied the family. They also took their dog, Tarzan. They traveled using a Packard motor carriage, an Overland delivery car, and a trailer. Ed kept a complete diary of their trip.

The Burroughses traveled to California again in 1916.

From the beginning, their adventure seemed to be doomed. At South Bend, Indiana, the delivery car could hold up no longer. Ed purchased a new Republic truck to replace it. By July 15, the group learned of an infantile paralysis epidemic along the east coast. They abruptly changed plans and decided to head for Los Angeles. They returned home to Chicago and waited until August 7 to begin the trek westward.

On September 12, Ed's forty-first birthday, the family was twelve miles west of Dodge City, Kansas. He recalled, "Twenty years ago this September 1st I rode south from Fort Grant, Arizona, with 'B' Troop of the 7th Cavalry after the Apache Kid and his band, and I was about as uncomfortable as I have been on this trip."

Driving through Ute Pass, Colorado, in search of a possible campsite, they had to push the truck up hills. Joan had taken ill, so they sought a doctor's help. Finally, Ed and Emma agreed that there would be no more camping. Ed wrote in his diary, "NEVER AGAIN! At least not with three little children. It is impossible to keep the flies away from them, the food is improperly cooked, and meals are irregular, cold and unpalatable...." Among the hazards were poisonous snakes.

Three months and nine days after their initial departure, the adventurers arrived in Los Angeles. They had traveled 6008 miles, 3527 of them between Chicago and Los Angeles. The trip did not help Ed's neuritis, but his overall health had improved, despite all the problems they encountered.

Chapter Six

Writing and Ranching

After the family arrived in Los Angeles, Ed rented a house for eight months and got back to work writing stories. The first one he finished was "The Son of Tarzan." Meanwhile, other stories were rejected. Davis and Sessions both rejected "Ben, King of Beasts" and "Beyond Thirty."

A book called *The Return of Tarzan* came out March 10, 1915, with a jacket illustration by the well-known artist N. C. Wyeth. Ed's next book contract was negotiated in October 1915 for *The Beasts of Tarzan* to be published in the forthcoming year. That same month, he finished "Tarzan and the Jewels of Opar." Some of his short stories appeared in *Blue Book* as "The New Tales of Tarzan," which would later be made into a book, *Jungle Tales of Tarzan.*

Los Angeles afforded Ed closer ties with the film industry. He reached an agreement with William Parsons of National Film Corporation to produce a silent movie of "Tarzan of the Apes." Ed would get $5000 cash,

$50,000 in capital stock, and five percent of receipts. The project looked good on paper, but it soon faltered. Ed was worried that the screenwriter would change the story. To convince Parsons that this would be a mistake, Ed devised a campaign to poll fans regarding how they wanted the movie shaped. This created tension between Ed and Parsons. Ed lacked trust in the movie venture so much that he sold his $50,000 worth of stock for $5000. When the opening of the film was scheduled in New York City in January 1918, he refused to attend.

Parsons went on with a second Tarzan film without authorization from Ed. Eventually relations between the two men became so difficult that Ed had a friend contact Parsons to patch things up. The two men agreed to speak in person. Parsons offered a $2500 advance on the new film. Ed was disappointed when *The Romance of Tarzan,* was released in 1918. It had been thrown together hastily and did not follow Ed's book at all. Many fans thought that Tarzan had become too civilized.

In 1916, the nation looked ahead to possible war with Germany, and forty-one-year-old Ed wanted to see military action. He enrolled in the Los Angeles Riding Academy to prepare for service. He also appealed to both General Charles King and Major General Frederick Strong, his commandants at Michigan Military Academy, for letters of recommendation to the Officers Reserve Corps. In all, he collected thirteen letters of recommendation, and his commission was granted.

The U. S. entered war with Germany in April 1917. In June, Ed and his family returned to Chicago, and he was notified that his commission as captain in the Illinois "reserves was issued as of July 19, 1917, Company A, Second Infantry."

Ed began writing to support the war effort. He prepared three articles of 400 words each–"To the Mother," "To the Home Girl," and "To the Woman on the Town." The last one advised prostitutes to help soldiers by leaving them alone when they were on leave in large cities. Ed sent these unsolicited articles to a syndication firm and asked that they be distributed.

In April or May 1918, Ed rented office space in Oak Park. He intended to use his office as a place to write, but he often used it to recruit men for the militia. In August 1918, he trained with his unit at Camp Stever, Illinois. When he returned home in September, he was promoted to major, commanding the First Battalion, Second Infantry of the Illinois Reserves.

He continued to write patriotic, and very anti-German, articles. The boy who once had difficulty adjusting to army discipline was now the man who urged others to support the war cause by buying Liberty Bonds and enlisting. He roused his readers by targeting Germans: "Each and every one of us pines to go over the top and spear a Hun.... Next to sticking a bayonet through a Hun's gizzard, you can inflict the greatest pain upon him by jabbing him in the pocket-book....watching the home

Boche wriggle when you get his purse pinned down."

Because of his age when the war started, Ed never saw action. He felt guilty enough over this to withdraw from active involvement in the Military Order of the Loyal Legion of the United States. In a letter to the organization, he said, "I now feel that to wear the insignia of the legion...is equivalent to assuming...honors...worn by another man."

McClurg scheduled publication of the books *The Return of Tarzan*, *The Beasts of Tarzan*, *The Son of Tarzan*, *A Princess of Mars*, *Tarzan and the Jewels of Opar*, and *The Gods of Mars* over a four-year period. The company paid the artist J. Allen St. John to illustrate the Tarzan books. Ed also published shorter works in 1918, including the novellas "The Land That Time Forgot," "The People That Time Forgot," and "Out of Time's Abyss." All three were set in prehistoric times and explored the idea of evolutionary progression. They also had a stout dose of anti-German sentiments.

Ed became restless again. He was tired of writing Tarzan stories. He decided he wanted to become a farmer in California. He developed a plan for a permanent move to Los Angeles by February 1918. The family intended to carry with them their two canaries and the Airedale terrier, Tarzan. The Packard and all furniture would be shipped.

Upon arriving in Los Angeles, Ed began searching for a farm. The 540-acre country estate of the late General

Harrison Gray Otis, publisher of the *Los Angeles Times*, was available. The house itself sat on a fifteen-acre hill. Although it cost more than he could easily afford, Ed was determined to have this picturesque ranch. He agreed to a price of $125,000. He planned to raise hogs on the property and, of course, leave plenty of time for horseback riding. He called his new ranch Tarzana.

Besides the idyllic life of a farmer, one of Ed's main reasons for the move to California was to be closer to the film companies. A man named Craft approached him to do a film of "The Return of Tarzan." He agreed, as long as Craft confined himself to use material only found in that story and not dip into his other Tarzan tales. Ed wanted to make sure he had plenty of opportunities to make more Tarzan movies. Ed would get $50,000 in stock, five percent of gross receipts, and $5000 cash. He also demanded that he would be co-director. But soon, he and Craft were fighting over filming. In the end, the film turned out to be quite different from the book and left Ed disappointed.

At the same time, Ed was preoccupied with problems of running the ranch and his other businesses. Even so, he kept writing and developed a story based on the German military campaign in Africa. Joseph Bray, his McClurg editor, advised Ed to downplay his animosity toward Germany, but Ed remained determined to portray Germans negatively. He wrote back, attempting humor, "...there ain't no such thing as a good German record."

Ed received bad news. His mother was terminally ill. She moved to Tarzana and for a while worked with a representative of the Christian Science church in the hope of healing herself. Eventually a doctor determined that she had a serious heart condition. In addition, she had a tumor on her kidney. She died in April 1920, at age seventy-seven.

For Christmas 1920, the National Film Corporation brought unusual gifts to the Burroughs: Two lion cubs and two monkeys. The cubs were young enough to be an endless delight for the children, but the monkeys proved difficult to control. Ed had to find them a new home.

Around this time, Ed and Emma decided to take their children out of public school. They were concerned that public schools would expose their children to disease. Jack had already had a serious bout with diphtheria. Nonetheless, Ed wondered if they always did the right thing for their children:

> I suppose we are bringing them up all wrong and that they will go to the damnation bow-wows because we don't beat them with sticks and make them go to schools where they are unhappy, but I have an idea that if a child doesn't get a great deal of happiness during its childhood it will never get it....

Ed brought many improvements to the ranch. He had

Ed called his 540-acre ranch "Tarzana."

a new central heating system installed. He erected a new building that housed a garage, servants' quarters, darkroom, workshop, and study (later to be used as a schoolroom). Beneath the building was a combination ballroom and movie theater. Every Friday night, Ed showed silent movies for his family, friends, and neighbors.

That same year, Ed had a swimming pool installed. He designed and supervised its construction. At the time, filtration equipment did not exist, so the pool had to be drained and refilled periodically to keep it clean. Ed and his children developed a custom of diving in for a quick swim on cold mornings.

The Burroughs residence became a social-gathering place on weekends. Regardless of the newly established Eighteenth Amendment prohibiting the sale or consumption of alcohol, parties were held, complete with drink and good food. Both Ed and Emma enjoyed having cocktails, but Emma found it difficult to control her intake of liquor. Once, frustrated by her behavior, Ed poured all the booze into the swimming pool and declared an end to weekend entertaining. This pronouncement did little to change Emma's drinking habits.

With all his elaborate spending, the ranch lost money. Neither the hogs nor the crops proved profitable. He rented out the farming portion of his estate. Although his writing income for 1921 was a handsome $98,238, he hadn't managed his expenses well. He got the idea to raise money by selling lots for real-estate development. He also tried getting movie studios to use his land for filming locations. All of the farm equipment and most of the livestock were sold at an auction in January 1923.

On March 23, 1923, Ed incorporated his business interests and formed Edgar Rice Burroughs, Incorporated, (ERB, Inc.). His family members were awarded stock shares, and Ed became a salaried employee of the corporation.

Shortly before incorporating, Ed decided to found a town called Tarzana and attempted to establish a post office with that name. This would make it easier for him to sell the lots. The community would vote to adopt the name Tarzana in July 1928, and a post office was established in December 1930.

Ed had lost interest in the Tarzan books. He felt he had no more to say about the subject, and besides, he did not want to be known only as the creator of Tarzan. He continued to receive pressure from his editors to pump out the same old stories. Readers, they said, were hungry for more Tarzan and more Martian chronicles, too. In 1922, he tackled the Tarzan idea again—this time with "Tarzan and the Golden Lion," which he began in February and completed at the end of May. He wondered how many more Tarzan adventures he had in him.

Chapter Seven

Controversy

A new moneymaking scheme presented itself to Ed—the development of his ranch into a country club. The Burroughs house would become the club headquarters. It was to be called El Caballero Country Club, and the goal was to make it the finest and most exclusive country club on the pacific coast. Soon, he was busy as a developer. In a letter to his brother Harry, he described his activities:

> Put unsold lots on the market myself...concluding a $200,000 bond issue by Edgar Rice Burroughs, Inc....completed laying eleven miles of pipe in the golf course in El Caballero...reopened the clubhouse the first of April...feeling that I have too much time on my hands I have recently taken an option on 120 acres close to the heart of town and am arranging to promote a public golf course...between times I am trying to exercise five saddle horses,

keep up my reading, and work for the interest of the saddle horse and bridle trail promotion here.

Ed's books were now being translated into twenty-one foreign languages. One estimate was that in the United States, Great Britain, Sweden, Germany, Hungary, Denmark, and Norway, about six million copies of Burroughs novels sold.

In Germany, however, the anti-German propaganda he had written during the war cooled the demand for his books. Ed lamely attempted to excuse himself by explaining that he did not dislike any particular nationality, rather he characterized villains from countries where he would be likely to have the fewest readers, so as not to offend the majority. Once readers from those countries began to emerge, he claimed he advised editors to change the offensive characters' nationalities. He said that he had offered this advice four years before the German upset. Ed's German publisher suggested that his next Tarzan story redeem the Germans and that Burroughs write an article showing how much he liked Germans.

In February, his German publisher telegraphed, "German Tarzan editions now much attacked by our press. Give us quickly good notices that...*Tarzan the Untamed* was born during war-bitterness and most of all that you are fond of German people...." Ed did as requested, but his apology had little effect. Purchases of his books virtually halted. Both his German editor and publisher suggested that at the root of this rebellion was the German press. They said the press was deeply jealous of Ed's success in its country, and it had manipulated German opinion against him. In one last attempt to make things right, Ed directed that all copies of both *Tarzan the Untamed* and *The Land That Time Forgot* be withdrawn from global circulation.

Davis had a new idea for Ed. He wanted Tarzan to confront a race of miniature people. Ed thought he had a better idea in Tarzan's visit to Abyssinia, where at that time there was an actual emperor with attendant warriors. Undaunted, Davis still argued for the little-people idea, with the added suggestion that Ed make each person two feet tall. Ed dropped the Abyssinia idea to focus on the little people. "Tarzan and the Ant Men" took five months to complete. His Minunians stood eight inches tall. In this work he consciously strove to remain objective, avoiding the mistake of prejudice apparent in earlier works.

Ed's prejudices and attitudes towards racial groups, and his ideas on evolution and genetics, played a big part in his fiction. Many of the characters and animals that populate his science-fiction stories are based on his understanding of how other life forms may have evolved under different conditions.

Ed was also a proponent of eugenics, the science which studies the factors that influence the hereditary qualities of a race, and more notoriously, how to improve a race. While covering a sensational murder trial for the

Los Angeles Examiner, he wrote that the murderer, who was pleading innocent by reason of insanity, should be executed not only for his crime but also because "moral imbeciles breed moral imbeciles, criminals breed criminals, murderers breed murderers just as truly as St. Bernards breed St. Bernards." He went on to say that executing the murderer of this crime would not be enough. "The city [Los Angeles] has plenty of moral imbeciles that we might well dispense with...destruction and sterilization are our defense and we should invoke them while we are yet numerically in the ascendancy."

Ed was attacked for these articles. His editors advised him to rein in his opinions, and he agreed to try. But, try as he might, his strong opinions and prejudices crept into his work. In "Marcia of the Doorstep" he created a negative, stereotypical picture of radicals and communists. In more than one spot he had characters poke fun at "Bolsheviks" (the informal name of the Soviet Communist leaders), the union group International Workers of the World, and women's rights.

From November 1923 to April 1924, Ed worked on a steady flow of books for McClurg: *At the Earth's Core* (1922), *The Chessmen of Mars* (1922), *Tarzan and the Golden Lion* (1923), *Pellucidar* (1923), and *The Land That Time Forgot* (1924). He completed "Marcia of the Doorstep" in October 1924.

In May 1925, Ed finished the third of his Mars series, "The Red Hawk," and in November, he completed "A

Weird Adventure on Mars." This story introduced a new character, Ulysses Paxton. It also had references to organ transplants and included the invention of an individual flying machine smaller than an airplane.

The next few years were a whirlwind for the Burroughs family. First, they moved to Los Angeles proper. In 1926, they returned to Tarzana, to a seven-room cottage adjoining the residence-now-turned-clubhouse. Ed had other rooms added to the cottage, but the new residence was so small that he relocated his office to another building in the town of Tarzana. In time, this would become the headquarters of ERB, Inc. Ed was in his new office by July 1927. Eventually, he was forced to foreclose on the unsuccessful El Caballero club, which gave him back his former residence, garages, stables, and other outbuildings. He now owned 345 of the original 550 acres.

The country club and public golf course were not his only mistaken business ventures. In 1929, he invested in the construction of the ill-starred Los Angeles Metropolitan Airport. That same year he sank funds into a company that manufactured airplane engines. He thought aviation was a safe bet. But, on the eve of the Great Depression, the company's prototype failed an important federal test, which meant that the engine could not go into production. In 1931, the airport project folded.

Ed's two sons enrolled in Urban Military Academy in Los Angeles. But by 1924, having found the military regimen unsatisfactory, they opted for public school; and

From left to right, Joan, Hulbert, Edgar, Emma and John Burroughs.

in 1926, they began attending the Los Angeles Coaching School, noted for its small classes and special instruction. In the fall of 1928, Hulbert was at Van Nuys High School. Jack followed him there the next year. One year later, Hulbert went to Pomona College in Claremont. Again, Jack followed behind him the next year. Jack graduated from Pomona in 1934 *magna cum laude* with distinction in the field of art. Eventually, Jack became a sports writer, although he disliked the work. After graduation from college, Hulbert went to the University of New Mexico summer school of archeology. He became a photographer.

Daughter Joan wanted to become an actress. She attended various acting schools. Afterward, she worked with a stock company. When the company dissolved because of financial problems, she returned home to work with the Menard Players at Glendale Playhouse. During the summer of 1926, she met Jim Pierce, who was a former All-American football player from the University of Indiana and the coach at Glendale High School.

Joan invited Jim to a pool party at her parents' home. Ed saw his tanned skin and muscular frame and had the idea that Jim Pierce might make a good Tarzan. He arranged a screen test and Pierce starred in *Tarzan and the Golden Lion*. This film became the first full-length Tarzan feature and the last of the Tarzan silent movies.

On the set for *Tarzan and the Golden Lion*, Ed was not pleased with the way things were going. He suggested changes, which went ignored. Boris Karloff had a small role as a Waziri chief. Joseph Kennedy (father of the famous president and two senators) owned the distribution rights. The film did poorly, which Ed claimed was the result of "poor direction and rather stupid cutting."

Joan and Jim Pierce became engaged in July 1928 and married in August at the Burroughs residence. After the failure of the movie *Tarzan and the Golden Lion*, possibilities for Jim Pierce to find full-time movie work were limited. Pierce moved on from Glendale High School to become the football coach at the University of Arizona.

The 1920s and 1930s were times of illness for Ed and Emma. In 1923, Emma had to have her appendix removed. Two years later she had gall bladder surgery. Later, she suffered from arthritic pain. Ed worked himself to the point of exhaustion. In 1924, he was excused from jury duty because of heart pain. In March 1930, he experienced abdominal pain. The problem was a bladder obstruction, which caused him to visit the hospital on four different occasions and undergo two minor operations.

Emma's alcoholism progressed and her drinking became a serious problem in their marriage. Ed hated what alcohol was doing to his marriage, and his novels reflected an intolerance for excessive drinking. Yet, in May 1927, Ed joined the Association Against the Prohibition Amendment. He wrote to its executive secretary, "I am just one of the many who believe that any tendency on the part of the Government to interfere in the purely personal conduct of the life of an individual citizen is more dangerous than the evil it is intended to eradicate."

Chapter Eight

Success and Failure

Ed was productive during the last years of the 1920s and into the 1930s. After he completed "Tarzan, Lord of the Jungle" in 1927, he went on to write eight more works of fiction, including three more Tarzan books. He also exercised every morning. He rode horses and walked in the countryside. He enjoyed playing cards and reading nonfiction books, and spending time with his children.

The Pellucidar saga had not been updated for fourteen years. Reader requests led Ed to write a 1928 sequel called "Tanar of Pellucidar." Another sequel in 1929 was originally called "Tarzan and Pellucidar" but was later retitled "Tarzan at the Earth's Core." It became a seven-part series in *Blue Book* from September 1929 to March 1930. "A Fighting Man of Mars," rejected by *Argosy* and *All-Story*, was accepted by *Blue Book*. The new editor of *Blue Book*, Kennicott accepted "The Land of Hidden Men."

The stock market crash and ensuing Great Depression idled over a third of America's workforce. Initially, Ed did not suffer any ill effects. The Tarzan books had been turned into comic strips that were syndicated to over a hundred newspapers. This provided him with a new source of income and helped to keep the Tarzan brand before the public.

Inevitably, however, the economic malaise began to cut into book sales. Ed was anxious to find some way to increase revenues. The obvious place to look was Hollywood. He received a call from the largest, most successful movie studio of them all. Metro-Goldwyn-Mayer wanted to make a "talkie," a sound movie, with the Tarzan character. They wanted to create their own story, not follow his plots. The giant studio, home of such stars as Clark Gable and Greta Garbo, did promise to use authentic footage of Africa that had been shot for an earlier movie. This meant that many of the scenes would have the look and feel of Africa.

Another good omen was the actor selected to play Tarzan. Earlier actors, including Ed's son-in-law, Jim Pierce, had seemed wooden and self-conscious playing an ape-man dressed in the skimpy costume. The new Tarzan was one of the most famous athletes of his day, Olympic gold medal swimmer Johnny Weismuller. Weismuller was able to carry off the role with a naturalness that has continued to make him the most recognizable of the several actors who have attempted the part. Maureen O'Sullivan played the role of Jane.

In 1932, the studio released *Tarzan the Ape-Man*. It was such a success that *Tarzan and His Mate* was released in 1934. A radio serial of "Tarzan of the Apes," starring Ed's daughter, Joan, and her husband, Jim Pierce, began broadcasting in 1932.

At last Ed's long-neglected work *The Outlaw of Torn* was published as a book by McClurg. Since 1917, McClurg had published at least two Burroughs books a year. As of September 1927, total Edgar Rice Burroughs book sales in the United States and Great Britain came to 6,355,000 copies.

Ed got the idea to use the success of Tarzan to market other products, and soon ERB, Inc. was overseeing the production of Tarzan Bread, Tarzan Ice Cream Cups, and Tarzan Belts. By 1939, twenty-six companies were handling various Tarzan items, including small clay figures that were the precursor of today's "action figures." The company also organized Tarzan Clans of America, a group similar to the Boy Scouts.

Ed did not want to share his book profits with a publishing company. He decided to create a publishing division of ERB, Inc to publish his own works. Whatever the enterprise, Ed always sought ways to increase his profits.

Ed's career as a writer and an entrepreneur reflected an important aspect of his personality. One part of him was very social and craved the company of others; the other side was private and craved the solitude of the countryside. One reason for the privacy was to hide an unpleasant truth from outsiders. For years, Ed and Emma

Johnny Weismuller and Maureen O'Sullivan remain the most memorable movie Tarzan and Jane.

had given the impression that theirs was a perfect marriage. But what most outsiders did not know, and the three children knew well, was that the marriage had become one in name only. Emma's alcoholism had torn them apart.

Ed had actually left home more than once, but he always returned. Now the children were grown and his tolerance gone.

In 1927, Ed had begun working on a film project with the producer Ashton Dearholt. Dearholt's wife, Florence, accompanied him during some of their meetings. She had been an actress before she gave up her career to devote herself to raising their two children.

While Ed and Ashton were working on their project, Florence befriended Ed's daughter, Joan. On several occasions, the Burroughses and the Dearholts met socially. While Ashton was on location in Guatemala for RKO Studios, Ed took his first vacation without Emma. He called this his "thinking trip." He returned refreshed, but the situation with Emma remained the same. Then, fifty-eight-year-old Ed decided to learn how to fly a plane. His diary entry for January 5, 1934, read, "First flying lesson today about noon." He used the name "Smith" when registering for the lessons because he wanted to spare Emma worry, but she learned about them anyway. He eventually purchased a plane, performed his first solo flight, and got his wings. "Great thrill," he noted in his diary.

Two new diary entries for February 1934 hinted at the dramatic change in his life:

> February 20: Came to live at The Garden of Allah, Villa 23.
> February 26: ...went to Palm Springs with Florence.

During the ensuing months, Ed and Florence Dearholt became entangled in a rather unusual relationship. While Ed and Florence began a love affair, Ashton Dearholt began a relationship with actress Ula Holt. The four often met for dinner. In March, the Dearholts divorced. By the end of March, Florence and Ed saw each other daily.

Meanwhile, Ed's business ventures required some decisions. Ashton Dearholt wanted Ed to become partners in a new film company, Burroughs-Tarzan Enterprises (BTE). Their first project, using actor Herman Brix as Tarzan, was *The New Adventures of Tarzan.* It was to be a serial in twelve episodes filmed in Guatemala.

On October 21, 1934, Ed moved to Las Vegas to satisfy a six-week residency requirement necessary before he could attain a divorce from Emma. The divorce was granted December 6. After Florence's divorce became final, the two were married April 4, 1935, in Las Vegas. Ed was sixty; Florence was thirty. They honeymooned in Honolulu. While there, she took her first swimming lesson. Ed, trying to keep up with his much younger wife, took his first surfing lesson. Ashton eventually married Ula Holt, who had a role in *The New Adventures of Tarzan*. Both Ed and Ashton remained close and continued their business relationship.

Once the couple had returned to Los Angeles after their Honolulu honeymoon, they moved to various places. First, they rented a home in Palm Springs for eight months and spent most of their time playing tennis. Ed even helped organize the Palm Springs Tennis Club. Ed and Florence moved back to Los Angeles in May 1936, moving from apartment to apartment before settling for a short while in Hollywood.

Ed expressed his love for Florence in a unique way. The prologue title and chapter titles of *The Swords of Mars* (1936) are arranged so that the first letters make up an acrostic: "To Florence with all My Love Ed."

The nineteenth Tarzan sequel was written between May 1934 and January 1935. *Blue Book* took it for $3000, giving it the title "Tarzan and the Immortal Men."

Ed now had a new illustrator—his son Jack. Jack would illustrate thirteen Burroughs books in all. J. Allen St. John did his final illustrating job in the fall of 1936 for *Tarzan's Quest*.

Ed wrote his fifth Pellucidar serial, "Back to the Stone Age," between January and September 1935. Although he took eight months to write it, the story was not up to his old standards, perhaps because of his divorce and new marriage. Eventually, *Argosy* accepted the serial for

Ed married Florence Dearholt on April 4, 1935.

$1500. Called "Seven Worlds to Conquer," it ran in six parts between January and February 1937.

The sequel to "Tarzan and the Magic Men" was "Tarzan and the Elephant Men," written between December 1936 and March 1937. This later became the last half of the book *Tarzan the Magnificent*, published in September 1939.

Ed was losing some of his muscle with publishers. Some editors thought that his stories were not fresh enough. There had been a huge surge of new pulp magazines. Most specialized in a specific genre, such as mystery or science fiction. New writers, such as Robert Heinlein in science fiction and Raymond Chandler in detective stories, began publishing fiction that did not depend on last minute coincidences or superhuman feats. As Tarzan gained new popularity on the screen, he began to lose some of his dominance as a fictional character among readers. Nevertheless, Ed continued to self-publish, and soon ERB, Inc. re-introduced *The Lad and the Lion*, adding 21,000 words to make it stretch into book length. Unfortunately, this created considerable repetition and made the two subplots appear unconnected.

"The Synthetic Men of Mars" was completed in August 1938. Byrne of *Argosy* called it his best work in five years. Ed had risen to the challenge presented by the new wave of science fiction, creating an imaginative example of that genre. Unlike most of his stories, Ed spent seven months writing it.

Ed wrote an article about lions called "Man-Eaters" that was serialized in six parts in the *New York Evening World*. One recollection Ed had was of a particularly confused lion. Crewmembers used whips and blank guns to try to get the lion to move, which upset him. He leaped a fence and headed toward Ed and his young daughter Joan. Fortunately, the animal was too frightened to attack, and trainers soon had him caged. At a Los Angeles zoo, the story was tragic rather than comical. A lion was scheduled to jump onto a man. To make the lion jump electric shock was used. This angered the lion, and he killed the man. "Man-Eaters" first appeared in the *Sunday Magazine* of the *Los Angeles Times* on August 22, 1937.

Another article, "The Author-Publisher," appeared in a 1937 issue of *Writer's Digest*. In the article, Ed explained that his reason for turning to the publication of his own books was greed. Back when he had negotiated his contracts with publishers, he had pushed for high royalties. This created a very small profit margin, which discouraged publishing companies from pushing sales. Thus, he had turned to self-publishing. He admitted that if he had been less greedy, he might not have found it necessary to self-publish.

Ed and Dearholt's BTE had suffered from the beginning. Neither Dearholt nor Ed were experienced enough as producers to make it succeed. BTE did manage to produce mediocre versions of *Tarzan Escapes* (1936), *Tarzan Finds a Son* (1939), *Tarzan's Secret Treasure*

(1941), and *Tarzan's New York Adventure* (1942).

People close to Ed began to die. General Charles King, his commandant at the Michigan Military Academy, died in 1933. Joseph Bray, president and board chairman of A. C. McClurg and Company died in 1939. In 1940, Ed's brother Harry passed away.

Ed's new social life was so demanding that it interfered with his writing. Time was not the only price he paid for the time away from his desk. He felt the pinch financially. He reasoned moving to Hawaii with his new wife and her two young children might save money. Typical of his impulsive moves, he packed up his new family's belongings, and they sailed for the Hawaiian Islands.

Despite problems with insects and rodents in the tropical climate, Ed bought a new Dictaphone, secured the services of a typist, and resumed writing work in earnest. His new approach was to separate work from home life and not discuss his story ideas with his family. He maintained his regular writing schedule, but social affairs still filled his evenings. Among other distractions, he developed a fondness for playing bridge.

Chapter Nine

Hawaii

In 1940, ERB, Inc. published *The Synthetic Men of Mars* and *The Deputy Sheriff of Comanche County* with illustrations by John Coleman Burroughs. After these, no Burroughs books came out until *The Land of Terror* in 1944 because of wartime paper shortages.

Amazing Stories published "The City of Mummies," "Black Pirates of Barsoom," "The Yellow Men of Mars," and "The Invisible Men of Mars"—all in 1941. These would become the book *Llana of Gathol* in 1948, the last book illustrated by John Coleman Burroughs. In all, Ed wrote eleven Martian novels.

Ed laid plans for a book about a new planetary system. He set up political and legal structures, ones complementary to his sense of justice. He wrote more than eight pages of background material in preparation for the series, including a glossary, statistics, maps, and an alphabet. He planned that the series would revisit the regimes of Hitler and Stalin, but using a fictional approach. "Beyond the Farthest Star" was the beginning of this series.

Ed's new marriage became troubled. He missed his own children back in Los Angeles. To compensate, he threw himself into the Hawaiian social life. It was almost as if he and Florence reversed roles: Whereas in Palm Springs, Florence had pulled him along into the nightlife, in Honolulu he pulled her along. His drinking increased to the point where Ed was drunk every night. In time, he became abrupt with her children. For her part, Florence became upset when she realized Ed didn't have as much money as she had thought he had.

On March 14, 1941, Florence sailed back to California with her two children. While Ed publicly denied that her leaving was anything more than a visit home, privately he knew better. His diary entry for March 27 read: "Had a very bad night last night from worry about Florence and finances. Early this morning when I awoke I thought I had had a slight stroke in my sleep...."

He withdrew from society. Each day he went to a movie, then at night he went to bed early. He often went for days without speaking to anyone. He lost weight. He worried about finances.

Ed suffered from a urinary infection that required occasional hospitalization. Meanwhile, back in Los Angeles, Ed's children had gathered to decide how to help. Because Hulbert was the only one of them who was unmarried, he went to Hawaii. Hulbert was a welcome visitor. Father and son set up an exercise routine that made both feel better.

On the morning of December 7, 1941, Ed and Hulbert rose early to play a paddle-tennis match. They assumed the distant firing sounds they heard and the smoke they saw were the result of normal training exercises at Pearl Harbor and were impressed at the realistic exercises. When news came that the Japanese were bombing Pearl Harbor, they thought it was a rumor until a bomb exploded offshore not far from their hotel.

Just after noon, a call came for all men to report for emergency duty. Ed, Hulbert, and a friend joined up and were stationed on the wharf at the warehouse belonging to Tuna Packers Ltd. They were to stand guard between ten o'clock at night and two o'clock in the morning. At last, sixty-six-year-old Ed was part of military action.

Toward evening, Hulbert and Ed had to walk along a mile of roadway. Rain fell steadily. After midnight, they accompanied a group of Japanese being transported to another location. Back at the tuna plant, they had to sleep on a cement floor.

The next day during an alert, everyone on duty was to kneel or lie down to keep from being spotted by the enemy. But, Ed "...did no squatting nor lying down.... [I]f I once got down, I should never be able to get up again." At eight p.m. they were dismissed from duty.

A colonel asked Ed to write a daily column for the local newspapers and press services to enhance the war spirit. Ed titled his column "Laugh It Off." It lasted from December 1941 until January 1942.

Hulbert enlisted in the Army Air Corps as a photographer. Ed was then training with the Business Military Training Corps (BMTC). The commanding officer wanted Ed to be a public-relations officer. Ed advanced quickly through the ranks. On February 22, he was a corporal; two days later he was a second lieutenant.

Ed became concerned that the BMTC was being ignored by the regular armed services. He sought a more active role as a war correspondent. He was made a United Press representative in November 1942. His position was recognized by the army, but not by the navy. On November 30, he wrote an article on the year of martial law in Hawaii. His first trip as a war correspondent was to New Caledonia and Sydney, Australia, beginning December 24, 1942. He returned to New Caledonia January 10, 1943. Then he went back to Hawaii on the U.S.S. *Shaw*, a destroyer that had been damaged when stranded on a reef. He arrived back at Pearl Harbor on March 2, 1943.

Between March 1943 and January 1944, Ed wrote no fiction, but he did write several war-related articles. His detailed account of the war-correspondence trip covered sixty pages and was titled "The Diary of a Confused Old Man, or Buck Burroughs Rides Again."

Ed's months in the South Pacific had satisfied his wanderlust considerably. As he waited in vain for the army to send him into war zones again, he went back to "writing stories, corresponding with friends and relatives, and attending social functions."

Ed became a war correspondent in the South Pacific during World War II.

Some of Ed's early articles criticized the lenient treatment of Japanese Americans on Hawaii. Ed agreed with the idea of moving all 159,000 Japanese Americans who made their homes on Hawaii to relocation camps on the mainland. Many Japanese Americans had already been forced to leave their homes behind after the bombing of Pearl Harbor and resettle in the ramshackle relocation camps. As the war went on and he witnessed the sacrifices of the loyal Japanese, he became less stringent in his demand that the Japanese be interned. In an article published June 30, 1944, he admitted that he had found the majority of Japanese islanders to be "cooperative and courteous—as they have always been."

In March 1944, Ed was given permission to travel again—this time to the Gilbert Islands. On one of those islands he reunited with Hulbert, who was also on assignment there. Ed was back in Hawaii on April 24, 1944. He had flown 7000 miles on this last trip and had continued to write his war diaries.

Once back, he returned to his story writing, completing "Tarzan and the Foreign Legion" in September 1944. "Tarzan and the Foreign Legion" reflected his experience with the Japanese during his travels. As he had with the Germans during World War I, he portrayed the Japanese as villains. He also explained how Tarzan could remain eternally young by swallowing pills he had gotten during one of his adventures.

Happy and sad events occurred during 1947. On June 2, son Jack's wife gave birth to Ed's grandson Danton.

On June 8, Ed's brother George died in Fontana, California. Emma's drinking problem continued to worsen until she died of a stroke on November 5. To friends Ed confided, "It was a relief, as her condition was hopeless...." Both Hulbert and Ed were granted leaves to visit home. At the end of December, Ed had to undergo surgery for a hernia, which took him a month of recovery before returning to Hawaii.

Back on Hawaii in February 1945, Ed resumed writing his "Laugh It Off" column. He covered both Franklin Roosevelt's death and the VE Day celebration. After years of being a staunch Republican, Ed had highest praise for President Harry Truman, a Democrat.

After long withholding its approval of Ed as a correspondent, the navy finally granted him correspondence status. In May 1945, he left Pearl Harbor on the U.S.S. *Cahaba*. He was on the cruise for two months. At the end of this tour in July, he had flown 5000 miles and gone 11,000 miles by ship.

Not long after his return to Hawaii, Ed complained of chest pains. On August 10 came the announcement that World War II was officially over. On September 13, as he packed for a return to the mainland, he wrote in his diary, " I am having these attacks too frequently and wish I were home." He had to postpone his return home and be hospitalized for a month. At the end of October, he flew to California.

Back home, Ed rested. He wrote, "My life...consists in sitting. I tried to do something more strenuous the other day and had another heart attack; so I have taken up sitting again." At seventy-one years old, Ed tired easily because of the angina pectoris. His doctor also discovered arteriosclerosis. Ed started a story called "Xonthron" but never mentioned it after a diary entry. He also started another Tarzan story but gave it up after a few pages.

He kept up his correspondence with Caryl Lee, Florence's daughter. In January 1947, he picked her and her friend up at their school and drove the friend home. Then he took Caryl Lee home to lunch before driving her out to a horse ranch so they could see the palominos boarded there. The trip exhausted him

In August 1949, *The Cave Girl* was published as a paperback. Ed bought a new Buick Roadmaster coupe and his first TV set. Nearly every evening he watched sports. He gave up alcohol in December 1946 but returned to drinking in February.

Ed read a review in the *Los Angeles Examiner* of the film *Tarzan and the Huntress.* What he read shocked him: "Tarzan, impersonated by Johnny Weismuller, who has played the character eleven times, once again moves back to his original setting, the jungle, where the *late* Edgar Rice Burroughs first imagined him."

Ed wrote the newspaper about his puzzlement over the word *late*: "I have been an ERB fan for many years, and I am grieved to learn of his death. Will you kindly advise when, where, and under what circumstances it occurred."

He signed the letter, Edgar Rice Burroughs.

In 1948, Ed caused a three-car accident on Ventura Boulevard. His eyesight had been growing worse; he misjudged the speed and distance of the other cars. After that, he gave up driving altogether.

At the beginning of 1949, Ed admitted to his nephew Studley that he had not gotten a physical exam in almost three years. On March 4, his doctor told Ed he had Parkinson's disease, although Ed did not exhibit many of the symptoms.

In December 1949, Ed had another heart attack. It was a month before he was removed from oxygen. Then, on Sunday, March 19, 1950, seventy-four-year-old Ed had finished his breakfast and was sitting in bed going over the comic pages of the newspaper, when he died. He was alone. In keeping with his wishes, his body was cremated and his ashes buried next to his mother's under a favorite tree in front of the Edgar Rice Burroughs, Inc. offices.

Appendix

Legacy

Critics have attacked Burroughs on several fronts. A key complaint is that his style and control of language lack polish. Another criticism is lack of verisimilitude, or the inability to have the reader suspend judgment. At various times in his life Burroughs was accused of prejudice, particularly racism and sexism. Finally, critics have felt he relied too heavily upon formula writing.

Researcher Robert Greer broke Ed's plot formula down into an outline:

I. Introduction
    A. Main Character
    B. Transportation to another locale via ship, spacecraft, or supernatural means
II. Rising Action
    A. Situation where main character seems helpless
    B. Adoption or capture of main character
    C. Swift rise to leadership or power among the new society

III. Character Introduction
   A. Main character meets woman in distress
   B. Main character and woman fall in love
IV. Escape
   A. Main character and main female character escape from certain doom
   B. Main characters cross wilderness or trackless wastes
V. Loss
   A. Main character loses female main character through capture or misunderstanding
   B. Main character perseveres and regains companionship of female character
VI. Battle
   A. Main character forced into battle with forces of evil
   B. Main character, through victory, saves the planet, country, city, or society
VII. Conclusion
   A. Main character reunited with or weds female main character
   B. Main character praised or rewarded for his triumphs over conflicting forces

In the face of this criticism, a central question remains: How could a writer so lacking in polish attract so many readers? The scholar Erling Holtsmark took the same criteria used to criticize Burroughs and applied them to writers who had lived in ancient Greek and Roman times. Those writers, such as Sophocles and Euripedes, failed to meet the test as well. Holtsmark could only conclude that Burroughs was "a fine artist in his genre of heroic fantasy." He went on to show how Burroughs excelled in these categories: Language use, techniques, particularly employment of motifs, approach to the handling of animals in literature, the development of a hero, and treatment of themes.

Ed tended to stereotype characters more in his Tarzan books than in his non-Tarzan ones. He sometimes went way ahead of his colleagues in political correctness. Researcher Robert Hunton found his treatment of Native Americans in *The War Chief* commendable, claiming that their "deepest...needs for freedom and fairness are continuously reflected in the pages of ...[his] western masterpiece." Regarding Ed's tendency to reflect popular prejudices of his times, Thomas Gardner, speaking at the 1963 New York Science Fiction Association meeting said, "Burroughs had good Negroes and bad Negroes, good Jews and bad Jews, good Germans and bad Germans. He had good people and bad people of every kind in his books because there *are* good people and bad people of every kind."

An ongoing debate is whether Edgar Rice Burroughs should have written less and revised more. But, his goals were to make money and to entertain. Given the nature of the pulp market, he was forced to put quantity ahead of quality.

Ed often felt self-conscious about his lack of college

education and his shaky background in grammar. He covered this sensitivity with a mock-populist, braggadocio stance that included such deliberate misspellings as "damphool" and "litrachoor." The humorous front may have done as much to typecast him as editors did. Reviewers might well have responded to his bumpkin approach by coloring Ed a bumpkin in their reviews.

Whatever the final critical response to the fiction of Edgar Rice Burroughs will be, he did understand better than most of his colleagues what the mass of people enjoyed reading. Like all of us, he was a product of his times. He gathered ideas around him and tried to make the best life possible for his family. When in the bargain he was able to create entire worlds from his fertile imagination, we all benefited.

Glossary

academic—relating to school courses.

acrostic—composition in which initial letters of words or sentences spell a word or phrase.

angina pectoris—disease marked by brief, violent attacks of chest pain brought on by too little oxygen in the heart muscles.

arteriosclerosis—disease caused by abnormal thickening and hardening of the arterial walls, resulting in lost elasticity.

Boche—a derogatory term for a person of German descent.

classical—relating to ancient Greek or Roman times.

conciliatory—agreeable to compromise or appeasement.

disillusionment—the state of being left without hope or enchantment.

enticement—attraction by arousing hope or desire.

entrepreneurial—having to do with business or enterprise.

eugenics—science that deals with the improvement (as by control of human mating) of hereditary qualities of a race or breed.

first serial rights—copyrights relating only to the first time a work is published.

formula writing—writing in a prescribed or set form so that one plot resembles another.

frugal—a manner reflecting economy in the expenditure of resources; thrift.

gelding—castrated male horse.

gross receipts—receipts that do not include any deductions.

imminent—about to happen.

indigents—those suffering from poverty in which real hardship and deprivation are experienced.

indeterminate—not definite.

infringements—trespasses on rights or privileges.

Ivy League—relating to a group of long-established and widely respected eastern U.S. colleges.

motif—recurring thematic element in a work; dominant idea or central theme.

mythology—stories that embody a culture's morals, values, and beliefs.

ossify—change into bone.

Parkinson's disease—progressive nervous disease marked by tremors and muscle weakness.

precursor—one that precedes and indicates the approach of another.

pulp—magazine printed on newsprint or cheap paper, therefore less exclusive.

redeem—save or bring back from destruction.

reproach—express disappointment or displeasure.

scenario—sequence of events outlining the plot of a play.

scion—descendant or child.

sequel—next in a series.

serials—items appearing periodically rather than on a single date.

slick—magazine printed on glossy or more expensive paper, therefore more exclusive.

stereotype—to repeat without variation or make hackneyed; a standard mental picture held in common by group members.

subdivide—divide large land parcels into several smaller lots.

subdivisions—smaller lots formed when a large land parcel is divided.

syndication—the result of selling to a company that publishes in many newspapers or magazines at once.

verve—spirit and enthusiasm.

Suggested Reading

A Princess of Mars	1912
Tarzan of the Apes	1912
The Gods of Mars	1913
The Return of Tarzan	1913
The Warlord of Mars	1913
At the Earth's Core	1914
The Beasts of Tarzan	1914
The Outlaw of Torn	1914
The Mad King	1914
Pellucidar	1915
The Land that Time Forgot (trilogy)	1924
The Moon Maid (trilogy)	1926
The Pirates of Venus	1932
Lost on Venus	1933
The Deputy Sheriff of Comanche County	1940

Bibliography

Burroughs, Edgar Rice. *Autobiography*. (Unfinished and unpublished; retyped from original draft by George McWhorter, Curator, Edgar Rice Burroughs Memorial Collection, in 1985.) 1929.

ERBList. Online. Internet. Available Listserve: erblist@worldnet.att.net.

Fenton, Robert W. *The Big Swingers*. Englewood Cliffs, NJ: Prentice-Hall, Inc., 1967.

Holtsmark, Erling B. *Edgar Rice Burroughs*. Boston: Twayne Publishers, 1986.

————. *Tarzan and Tradition: Classical Myth in Popular Culture*. Westport, CT: Greenwood Press, 1981.

Hunton, Robert L. *"The War Chief* by Edgar Rice Burroughs: A Capsular Account of the Chiricahua Experience." *Burroughs Bulletin.* New Series 37. Winter 1999: 3-6.

Jeddak. com. Online. Internet. Available Web Site: http://www.jeddak.com.

Lupoff, Richard A. *Edgar Rice Burroughs: Master of Adventure.* New York: Canaveral Press, 1965.

Porges, Irwin. *Edgar Rice Burroughs: The Man Who Created Tarzan.* Provo, UT: Brigham Young University Press, 1975.

Taliaferro, John. *Tarzan Forever: The Life of Edgar Rice Burroughs.* New York: Scribner, 1999.

Tangor's Beyond.Online. Internet. Available Web Site: http://home.att.net/~bruce.bozarth.

Sources

CHAPTER ONE

p. 9, "I sneaked out of..." Burroughs, Edgar Rice. *Autobiography*. 1929, p. 9.

p. 10, "Your son deserted..." Burroughs, op. cit., p. 9.

p. 14, "I did chores..." Burroughs, op. cit., pp. 2-3.

p. 15, "Cadet Burroughs has made..." Porges, Irwin. *Edgar Rice Burroughs: The Man Who Created Tarzan*. Provo, UT: Brigham Young University Press. 1975, p. 33.

p. 16, "rifles at fifty paces" Porges, op. cit., p. 40

CHAPTER TWO

p. 20, "the worst assignment..." Porges, op. cit., p. 54

p. 21, "When they made..." Porges, op. cit., p. 56.

p. 21, "The muscles of those..." Porges, op. cit., p. 59.

p. 22, "If you think..." Porges, op. cit., p. 64.

p. 23, "My Wonderful Military Career" Porges, op. cit., p. 66.

p. 24, "After I had got..." Porges, op. cit., pp. 66-67.

p. 25, "I wish I could..." Porges, op. cit., p. 70.

p. 25, "God never..." Burroughs, op. cit., p. 43.

p. 28, "Stanley Basin..." Burroughs, Edgar Rice. "Auto biography." *Sunday Telegram* (Portland, Maine). 1933.

p. 30, "a blue uniform..." Porges, op. cit., p. 92.

p. 30, "I took all..." Burroughs. *Autobiography*, op. cit., p. 50.

CHAPTER THREE

p. 31, "expert accountant" Porges, op. cit., p. 94.

p. 32, "forthrightness, attitude..." Porges, op. cit., p. 95.

p. 33, "I would probably..." Porges, op. cit., p. 105.

p. 34, "There were several all-fiction..." Taliaferro, John. *Tarzan Forever: The Life of Edgar rice Burroughs, The Creator of Tarzan*. New York: Scribner, 1999, p. 60.

p. 34, "I had never..." Burroughs, *Autobiography*, op. cit., p. 55.

p. 35, "The story I am..." Porges, op. cit., pp. 123-124.

p. 38, "I find I can..." Burroughs, Edgar Rice. "Contact." *Hardware Mutual Casual Company*. 30 October 1939.

CHAPTER FOUR

p. 40, "Sorry you don't..." Porges, op. cit., p. 150

p. 41, "Father's birthday" Porges, op. cit., p. 153.

p. 41, "somehow your course..." Metcalf, Thomas. Letter to Edgar Rice Burroughs. 26 February 1913. Porges Papers. Edgar Rice Burroughs Memorial Collection, Ekstrom Library, University of Louisville, Louisville, KY.

p. 45, "I might say..." Porges, op. cit., p. 172.

p. 46, "...all manner of..." Metcalf, Thomas. Letter to Edgar Rice Burroughs. 12 January 1914. Porges Papers. Edgar Rice Burroughs Memorial Collection, Ekstrom Library, University of Louisville, Louisville, KY.

CHAPTER FIVE

p. 52, "folding beds..." Porges, op. cit., p. 238.

p. 54, "Twenty years ago..." Porges, op. cit., p. 247.

p. 54, "NEVER AGAIN!" Porges, ibid.

CHAPTER SIX

p. 57, "reserves was..." Porges, op. cit., p. 285.

p. 57, "Each and every..." Porges, op. cit., p. 288.

p. 58, "I now feel..." Porges, op. cit., p. 290.

p. 59, "...there ain't..." Porges, op. cit., p. 325.

p. 60, "I suppose we..." Burroughs, Edgar Rice. Letter to Harry Burroughs. 4 January 1921. Porges Papers. Edgar Rice Burroughs Memorial Collection, Ekstrom Library, University of Louisville, Louisville, KY.

CHAPTER SEVEN

p. 64, "Put unsold lots..." Burroughs, Edgar Rice. Letter to Harry Burroughs. 3 April 1925. Porges Papers. Edgar Rice Burroughs Memorial Collection. Ekstrom Library, University of Louisville, Louisville, KY.

p. 65, "German Tarzan editions..." Porges, op. cit., p. 394.

p. 67, "The city..." Taliaferro, op. cit., p. 230.

p. 71, "poor direction..." Burroughs, Edgar Rice. Letter to Cadet Herbert T. Weston, Jr. 18 April 1929. Porges Papers. Edgar Rice Burroughs Memorial Collection, Ekstrom Library, University of Louisville, Louisville, KY.

p. 71, "I am just one..." Porges, op. cit., p. 451.

CHAPTER EIGHT

p. 76, "thinking trip" Porges, op. cit., p. 558.

p. 77, "February 20..." Porges, op. cit., p. 559.

CHAPTER NINE

p. 84, "Had a very..." Porges, op. cit., p. 620.

p. 85, "did no squatting..." Taliaferro, op. cit., p. 338.

p. 86, "writing stories..." Porges, op. cit., p. 636.

p. 88, "cooperative and courteous..." Burroughs, Edgar Rice. "Our Japanese Problem." *Hawaii*. 30 June 1944.

p. 89, "It was a relief..." Porges, op. cit., p. 642.

p. 89, "I am having..." Porges, op. cit., p. 649.

p. 90, "My life..." Burroughs, Edgar Rice. Letter to Bert Weston. 1 May 1946. Porges Papers. Edgar Rice Burroughs Memorial Collection, Ekstrom Library, University of Louisville, Louisville, KY.

p. 90, "Tarzan, impersonated by..." Porges, op. cit., p. 695.

p. 90, "I have been..." Burroughs, Edgar Rice. Letter to the *Los Angeles Examiner*. 26 April 1947. Porges Papers. Edgar Rice Burroughs Memorial Collection, Ekstrom Library University of Louisville, Louisville, KY.

APPENDIX

p 92, "I. Introduction..." Greer, Robert. *From Africa to Mars: The Political, Moral and Social Commentaries of Edgar Rice Burroughs*. Thesis. Online web page. www.Jeddak.com.

p. 94, "a fine artist..." Holtzmark, *Tarzan and Tradion: Classical Myth in Popular Culture*, p. 6.

p. 94, "deepest...needs for" Hunton, Robert L. *"The War Chief* by Edgar Rice Burroughs: A Capsular Account of the Chiricahua Experience." *Burroughs Bulletin*. New Series 37. Winter 1999, p. 3.

p. 94, "Burroughs had good..." Lupoff, Richard, A. *Edgar Rice Burroughs: Master of Adventure*. New York: Canaveral Press, 1965, p. 163.

Index